Giver of Gifts

THREE STORIES
OF CHRISTMAS GRACE

Jerry Camery-Hoggatt

Revell
Grand Rapids, Michigan

© 2001, 2007 by Jerry Camery-Hoggatt

Published by Fleming H. Revell
a division of Baker Publishing Group
P.O. Box 6287, Grand Rapids, MI 49516-6287
www.revellbooks.com

When Mother Was Eleven-Foot-Four was previously published in 2001

Printed in the United States of America

Library of Congress Cataloging-in-Publication Data
Camery-Hoggatt, Jerry.
    Giver of gifts : three stories of Christmas grace / Jerry Camery-
Hoggatt.
        p.   cm.
    ISBN 10: 0-8010-3162-1 (pbk.)
    ISBN 978-0-8010-3162-5 (pbk.)
    1. Christmas stories, American. I. Title.
PS3603.A454G58 2007
813'.6—dc22   2007014947

For Bill and Lauren Younger,
givers of extravagant gifts,
agents of grace

CONTENTS

When Mother Was
Eleven-Foot-Four

1

This is the story of the Christmas of 1963, which is the Christmas that I learned what it means to be a giver of gifts. But this story isn't about me. This story's about my mother.

My mother's name was Josephine Mary Knowles Hoggatt, but everybody called her simply "the Lady," because in our town she was a woman of stature.

My mother was eleven-foot-four.

Okay, she wasn't eleven-foot-four *all* the time, just *some* of the time. She was eleven-foot-four when she needed to be. Most of the time she was four-foot-eleven. She was a tiny little woman—on the heaviest day of her life she weighed less than a hundred pounds—but she always said that when she was at her very best, she was eleven-foot-four.

Whenever she would say, "I drew myself up to my full height, and . . . ," we knew we were about to hear a story of some encounter in which she had demonstrated that even a person who was tiny on the outside could be large on the inside.

You should have seen my mother when she was eleven-foot-four.

This really happened: When Mother was in her sixties she ran a home for delinquent boys—"the Tujunga Ranch Home for Boys," she called it. It was my tiny, white-haired mother and fourteen juvenile delinquents.

One of the boys in the Tujunga Ranch Home was a tough little guy named C.J., whose older brother was a member of the Hell's Angels motorcycle gang. One Saturday morning my mother was awakened by the sound of banging on her front door and the revving of motorcycle engines in the driveway. When she went to the door to see who it was, there stood C.J.'s older brother, pounding on the door with the butt end of a bowie knife. To hear the boys tell the story later, C.J.'s brother was seven feet tall, tattooed everywhere, and wearing a way-too-small black T-shirt with a skull printed on the back.

He scowled at my mother. "Lady," he growled, "I'm giving you just ten minutes to get C.J. and all his stuff out here on the porch."

My mother looked C.J.'s brother straight in the eye and said, "Young man, I'm giving *you* just two minutes to get off my property." Then she drew herself up to her full height, looked *down* at him, and held her gaze steady.

He blinked first.

"Yes, ma'am," he said. With that, he turned around, climbed back on his motorcycle, and drove away. He took his gang with him, and Mother never saw him again.

After that, she never had any trouble with her fourteen juvenile delinquents either, but it wasn't because they had seen her stare down a Hell's Angel. Her boys didn't give her any trouble because they had all seen for themselves what my mother was like when she was eleven-foot-four.

My mother could be as tough as nails when she needed to be.

My father's name was William Hoggatt, but everybody called him by his middle name, Kelly. He was a tall, angular, good-looking man who didn't know he was good-looking. He wore a wide-brimmed gray felt hat pulled low over one eye, which gave him a rather rakish look. Sometimes he wore the collar of his shirt outside the collar of his sport coat. It was a look that eventually went the way of the big bands, but in the fifties it was high style, "genuine Savile Row," my mother said. More than once I saw my father turn the heads of married women as we made our way to our table at Bob's Big Boy restaurant after church.

I didn't know my father was good-looking either, but I can tell you when I found out: Mount Craig Summer Camp, 1961. I was eleven years old. My father was unloading our stuff from the back of the station wagon while we carried everything up to the cabin. From the door of the cabin I looked back, ostensibly to see how he was doing, but really to check out the girls. To my absolute astonishment, the girls were checking out my dad.

"Who was that man?" one of the girls asked as she watched my father drive away. I found out later her name was Leslie.

"That's my father," I said.

"You gonna grow up to look like him?" Leslie asked.

"That all depends. What do you think of my father?"

"I think your father is a very good-looking man," she said. There, it was out in the open.

"Well, then, in that case, I will," I said.

It didn't happen. I ended up favoring my mother, but Leslie never knew that. Before the week was over she had become the first girl I ever kissed. I suppose in my more honest moments I realize that I owe my father a debt of gratitude for that kiss, but I never told him. I don't think he would have approved. After all, I was only eleven.

William Kelly Hoggatt was a man of principle. His principles were always strange to me—sometimes they obligated him to do things that my principles now prohibit—but right now I want to honor the fact that he was measuring his life against a yardstick larger than his own vested interests. He charted his course by a compass outside himself, and he was absolutely committed to following whatever path that course required, never mind the consequences. Consequences were absolutely beside the point, he said.

If you had asked my father to list the virtues of a principled man, he would have told you that pride of place at the top would go to honesty and that running a close second place would be consistency. Now, that's a little odd, really. People don't usually think of consistency as a virtue, but it was for my father. For him, consistency was a theological virtue because *God* was consistent—"the same yesterday, today, and forever," he often said, "and anybody who wants to be like God should be consistent too."

The upside of my father's consistency was that he was absolutely reliable. If he said he would be somewhere, he would be there. If he said he would do something, he would do it. If he said he would cover some expense, you could trust that it would happen. He was dyed-in-the-wool, take-it-to-the-bank reliable, my father was.

There were two downsides to my father's insistence on living his life consistently. The first was that he was predictable. He didn't approve of surprises. He ran his whole life by the budget, the calendar, and the to-do list.

The second downside to my father's consistency was that he was inflexible. He didn't approve of compromise any more than he approved of surprises. Compromise meant not only that you were weak; it also meant that you had no scruples, no character. When I was ten years old, my father and I had an argument about some matter or another. As I recall, it had something to do with whether or not I could go horseback riding with some friends. I laid out my case. When I was finished, my father looked at me and said that I was right, my evidence was good, and my reasoning was logical, but his mind had already been made up, and he was going to stick with his original decision.

"If I change my mind now," he said, "you'll think you can change my mind about other things, and there'll be no end to the negotiating. I don't intend to spend my life bandying words with a ten-year-old!"

If my mother could be as tough as nails,

my father could be as hard as flint. He was the best and the worst of what it meant to be a realist. He was a realist, he said, because God is a realist.

But Mother was a romantic. Ask Mother for a list of virtues, and right at the top would be honesty—that much she shared with my father—but for her, right next to honesty came not *consistency* but *wisdom*.

My mother agreed with my father that there was an important place for the budget, the calendar, and the to-do list. It's important to carry your own weight, to pay your own way. "Keep your promises," she told us. "Be where you say you'll be. Live within your budget. Keep a stiff upper lip. Stay the course. Endure. Live within limits." One ought to do such things as a matter of course, she always said.

Except sometimes.

Sometimes, my mother said, you have to

set the calendar aside and hit the road with no destination, no map, and no deadline, and just see where the road takes you. "We'll just follow our nose," she would say.

Sometimes you have to set aside the to-do list and spend the day soaking up the afternoon sun. Or kick off your shoes and dangle your feet in a stream. Once she checked us out of school early to go fishing, not because she didn't respect school but because she wanted us to know firsthand that being industrious was only one part of living a good and full life.

She felt that way about the budget too. "Sometimes you have to set aside the budget and do something absolutely extravagant," she would say, "something your head tells you you can't afford but your heart tells you you can't do without."

Mother said that the ability to know when it was right to do such things was *wisdom*, and more than once she told us that the inner personal freedom to do something absolutely extravagant is the closest human beings ever come to understanding what God must feel when he is being gracious. This was especially so in the giving of gifts. According to Mother, when we give someone else an extravagant gift, we somehow rise above ourselves, even if only a little bit. We become better than we are, she said, larger on the inside.

My mother said she was a romantic because God was a romantic. She even had a romantic picture of what God looked like, to match his romantic character. The God in my mother's imagination had dark, wavy hair, longish and tossed back with flecks of gray at the temples, and a carefully trimmed black mustache. He had shockingly clear eyes. Mother said whenever she imagined God, he was wearing a black tuxedo with a red cummerbund, and a white silk scarf over his neck for style. Mother said that in her mind's eye God looked for all the world like Omar Sharif. (For my younger readers, my mother's God looked like Yanni with a haircut.)

Mother was a romantic because she believed in her heart of hearts that God was a romantic and that anybody who wanted to be like God should be a romantic too. That's the way she lived her life. When she turned sixty-three she sold the Tujunga Ranch Home for Boys and hit the road for the big adventure that had always filled her dreams. For more than a year we got postcards from Mother from all over the world—Europe, the Holy Land, Turkey. Once she wrote that she was living in a cardboard box in Mexico.

Before my mother died she told us she didn't want a funeral. "Invite everyone over and have a barbecue," she said.

She didn't want a hearse either. "Hire a

Dixieland band and dance my coffin to the cemetery," she said. In the end, we did have the barbecue, but we had a memorial service too, out of consideration for Mother's many friends. The only thing that prevented the Dixieland band was that she had decided at the last minute to have her remains cremated and thrown to the wind—a fitting symbol for the free spirit at the core of who my mother was.

Now, when you get two people as different as my mother and father, and as committed as they were to honesty—which they both took as the highest virtue—sparks fly. My mother and my father were champion arguers. They fought about everything. They fought about what we should wear to school. They fought about what color we should paint the house. They fought about whether or not we should admit Red China to the

United Nations. They fought about whether or not there should *be* a United Nations.

But there was absolutely nothing my parents fought about with greater passion or more intensity than the whole matter of Christmas gift giving. They didn't fight about what presents we should or shouldn't get; they fought about whether or not we should get any presents at all.

My father was opposed to Christmas gift-giving on principle.

2

We lived in a big, old, lumbering, three-story gray clapboard house that had at one time been a church. You could still see traces of the church in the structure of the building, like the paired windows on either side of the first floor where the sanctuary had been. The paired windows had been set up to correspond with the ends of the pews. The first floor had high ceilings and double doors that opened to what had been the church narthex.

Our family actually did its living on the second floor, where the parsonage had once been. There was a living room, a kitchen, my parents' room, a room for the girls, and a bathroom with a tub where we held family conferences. The third floor had been the church's attic, which my father finished off as a dormitory for the boys.

Eight children lived in the house—me, my sister, our three brothers, and our three cousins: Joyce, John, Jim, Jerry, Joel, Small Nathan, Vickie, and Pudge. Two girls. Six boys. Our cousins lived with us because our uncle Big Nathan was a single father, and he was in the navy and was stationed overseas for months at a time.

Between the second and third floors of the house my father had built a steep staircase, closed off on the bottom by a door. He intended the door as a way of closing off noises from the dormitory in the evenings when he and my mother entertained guests, but for us it served another purpose. The door meant we could slip down into the stairwell late at night in our pajamas and listen to our parents fight.

The fighting about Christmas presents always began sometime in early November. They had their moments, my mother and father, but these were the most colorful. Mother and Father—one an extravagant giver of gifts and the other a man of principle, one as tough as nails, the other as hard as flint, both committed to honesty as the first virtue, both determined to do what was right, neither one willing to compromise. The fights about Christmas presents were always terrifying and wonderful to hear.

Let me pause here and say that my father was not tightfisted in any sense. He was careful with his money, but within what he could afford he was a generous man. He made up for missing Christmas with a lavish pile of birthday presents, but he was opposed to

Christmas itself. He and my mother went at it every year, and it was always the same. The only things that changed from year to year were the intensity, the volume, and the determination they each showed not to lose this particular battle. The fights always ended with the same result, but it was never something we could take for granted, and so year after year we found ourselves in the stairwell, listening to our parents fight about Christmas.

We six boys would slip out of bed and sneak down the stairs and listen, afraid to breathe, knowing that how the argument turned out would determine how Christmas would be that year. Every November it went like this:

Mother started off. "Come on, Kelly. Sooner or later we're going to have to talk about the Christmas presents."

"Not this again," said my father. "You already know how I feel about all that."

"Maybe not. Maybe you've changed your mind somehow."

"Well, I haven't," said my father. (How could he change his mind? That would be inconsistent.) "Okay, I'll say it: I don't think we should give the children Christmas presents this year."

"Why not *this* time?" asked my mother.

"Christmas is too commercialized," said my father. "It's been taken over completely by the pagans. You know how I feel about that."

By "pagans" my father meant everyone who would make a buck on Christmas, and that included the atheists who sold things to Christians at a profit. And Jews. And Catholics. And Episcopalians, who were, after all, almost Catholic. And Lutherans. And Methodists. And Baptists. Mostly anyone who wasn't a Pentecostal.

My mother agreed with my father that

Christmas had been taken over by the pagans, but in her view we should take it back. Besides, she said, she didn't have any problem with someone making a buck on Christmas, so long as the buck was earned honestly and legally. "After all," she reasoned, "the people who make that buck will work hard for it. A lot of them will work overtime. They'll probably use it to pay the rent, or put food on the table, or buy Christmas presents for their own kids."

"It's bad business, mixing up Christmas with money," Father said. "People get all the wrong ideas about gifts and gift giving from doing that." He said what really stuck in his craw was the idea that you could somehow *earn* the gifts.

"Now, where would you get a cockamamy idea like that? And what on earth does any of that have to do with Christmas?" Mother wanted to know.

"You know exactly what it has to do with Christmas, Jo," said my father. "Santa Claus is out there keeping a list of who's naughty and who's nice. Giving gifts only to nice kids but cutting out the naughty ones. It messes up their understanding of what gift giving is all about. Turns the whole thing into a business transaction. Give a gift that way, and it's not a gift at all. It's payment for services rendered."

"Oh, for heaven's sake, Kelly, they're children." Mother's voice showed her exasperation. "They aren't going to go down that path. Only somebody who thinks like you would come up with reasoning like that. They don't think like you. Trust me on this one." Mother was growing impatient.

My father was growing impatient too. He said the bottom line was that he didn't want *his* kids growing up with the mistaken idea that there was anything at all about gifts and gift giving and Christmas that could be turned into a business transaction, giving in order to get, being good in order to get more presents, payment for services rendered.

Mother said she didn't want *her* kids growing up with the mistaken idea that if you wanted to find joy in your religion you had to convert and join the pagans.

When my father heard that, he knew he was in over his head, so he just flat-out pulled rank instead. "You don't understand, Jo," he said. "It's *my* decision. *I'm* the head of this house. *I* bring home the bacon, *I* write the bills, *I* put the bread on the table, and *I* decide whether or not there will be Christmas presents this year. As head of this house, I withhold permission." This final phrase—I withhold permission—was delivered slowly, ponderously, with an air of finality about it: "I . . . withhold . . . permission."

Behind the door, we six boys caught our breath. Even though I was too young to understand my father's argument, I knew from his tone that he was laying down the law. When Father laid down the law, it was nothing to be trifled with. How was Mother going to get past that? Everything depended on what she said next. In the silence we could feel more than hear, as our mother drew herself up to her full height. When she spoke, her tone had its own air of finality about it.

"No, Kelly," she said. "*You* don't understand. I'm not asking for permission. I'm inviting you to join me in signing the cards."

Behind the door, six young boys scurried up the stairs and back to bed. There would be Christmas. There would be presents. There was a God. God looked like Omar Sharif.

3

In the end, my father compromised with my mother, as he did every year. He always ended up compromising with my mother in three specific ways.

The first was that he allowed her to get a Christmas tree. He even put money in the budget for a six-foot tree. What he couldn't prevent was her habit of adding to the Christmas tree budget—what she called scrinching and sockofissing. She saved up nickels and dimes from the change at the Piggly Wiggly Market when she went grocery shopping. She horse-traded green stamps. I remember her doing the neighbor's ironing—sprinkling the shirts with a mixture of starch and water from a Coca-Cola bottle, then rolling them tight and storing them in the refrigerator until she could get to them late at night, after she had finished her own chores and put her children to bed.

Sooner or later, inevitably, she added enough money to my father's tree budget to buy a twelve-foot Christmas tree.

My mother bought her Christmas tree every year on the first Monday of December. She would do this on a weekday because my father was at work, and she knew it was hard for him. She always bought her tree from Ollie Flory, who ran the roadside peanut stand a mile up the highway. Every year Mr. Flory supplemented his income by setting up a Christmas tree lot next to his peanut stand. He always hauled the tree home for us in his truck, partly as a courtesy and partly because he took special delight in helping my mother turn this part of my father's Christmas philosophy on its head. Mr. Flory didn't much like my father. He always gave my mother a poinsettia plant to go with the tree—as a bonus for the big sale, Mother said, but we knew it was because my father would disapprove. Mother placed the poinsettia on the stairs with a sigh, I think because it reminded her that there were other romantics in the world. According to my father's definition, Mr. Flory wasn't a romantic. He was one of the pagans.

They started early because they had to "do the deed," Mr. Flory said, before my father got home. Mr. Flory would cut off an inch or so from the trunk of the tree and then some of the lower branches too, so my mother could scatter pine branches around the house and arrange candles among them. My mother said she loved the smell of pine needles in the house at Christmastime.

Then Mr. Flory and my mother and anyone else who was around would swing open
the wide double doors and muscle the tree
past what had been the narthex and into
the sanctuary. They had to set it up on the
first floor because that was the only place
in the house with high enough ceilings. It
was the only Christmas tree I ever saw inside
a house that had to be held in place with
guy-wires.

Then Mother decorated, standing on a
chair and starting with the popcorn strings.
The thing about popcorn strings is that you
have to pop the popcorn weeks early and
set it out so it can go stale. My mother had
strings of other things too—silver balls and
paper chains and cutout dolls—but she liked
the popcorn strings best, she said, because
they reminded her of the war years when
everybody had to make do or do without. She
said they reminded her of the Christmases

she spent praying for her brothers on the front or on ships all around the world, and how grateful she was that they'd all come home safe from the war.

Sometimes she added cranberries in among the popcorn to give a kind of red-white motif. She also added strings and strings of lights. She had strings of those big-bulbed colored lights that gave off a soft glow among the branches, and among these she added strings of tiny pinpoint white lights. Over the whole thing she scattered bits of that silvery tinsel that's supposed to look like icicles. She was always careful to scatter the tinsel where it would reflect the light from the strings of bulbs.

Then she got out her collection of ornaments. Some of her ornaments were ready-made. She and her brothers and her sister exchanged store-bought ornaments every year, and she traded ornaments with childhood friends and friends from the church, and over the years her collection had grown very large. In fine indelible ink on each one she wrote the date and the name of the person who had given it to her, and as she took them one by one out of their boxes she commented on the donors—how they met, why they were important, how long it had been since they had seen each other, what they had done that year, what hopes she had for them this year. Sometimes she just sighed. She was like an archaeologist, unearthing treasures from their crypts— boxes she kept in the large space beneath the stairwell. We learned our family history again every Christmas as Mother decorated her twelve-foot Christmas tree.

Among my mother's store-bought deco- rations were four little dancing girls, each with an opening to hold a tiny candle, and each with one of the letters of the word

N • O • E • L. (When Mother wasn't look-ing, my brother John always rearranged the letters to spell L • E • O • N instead.)

Far and away my mother's favorite orna-ments were the little handmade ones we brought home from Sunday school every year. She had hundreds of these tiny lit-tle ornaments made by unskilled, stubby children's fingers. There were pictures of her children pasted on cardboard backing and ringed about with glued-on Cheerios. There were little plastic baby Jesus figures glued into walnut half-shells—"the gospel in a nutshell," my Sunday school teacher had called them. There were "angels" made out of white paper plates with the wings cut out of the curve of the plates and the faces of her children pasted in where the faces of the angels should have been. There were handprints pressed into clay tablets, brought home from school, and when Mother hung them on the tree they weighed the branches down so low they brushed the floor. She had a whole collection of tiny stuffed toys, sent by a friend when my parents were newly married and had nothing besides popcorn strings for their first tree. She kept all these handmade Christmas decorations from year to year, and the collection of personal memories attached to them was a source of wonder to me.

If the glory of our house was my mother's twelve-foot Christmas tree, the crowning glory of the Christmas tree was her guardian angel. It was a twelve-inch doll she had inherited from her own mother. It had a finely detailed porcelain head and wings spread wide and a gossamer gown of antique lace.

My family followed the custom of allowing the youngest child in the house to place the angel on the tree as the final ornament, the *coup de grâce*. This presented a rather unique problem at our house. The youngest child in our family was my cousin Pudge. A twelve-foot tree has a wide circumference, and even when Pudge stood on a ladder he couldn't reach high enough or far enough to put the angel on the top branch.

My brother John solved this problem with a brass ring, a paper clip, and a fishing pole. He sewed the brass ring to the angel's dress right between the places where its wings connected to its shoulder blades. He made a hook from the paper clip and tied the hook to the fishing line. Then he simply lowered the angel into place like a crane operator. When the hook slipped out of the brass ring, Pudge threw the wall switch that turned on the lights, and then, all at once, magically, it was Christmas.

The neighbors would come for the evening, and we'd all drink wassail and cider and sing

Christmas carols. They would already be there when my father got home from work, so how could he object? I think he was always dazed a little by the change Mother's Christmas tree made in the atmosphere of the house. Even a realist has to admit the presence of magic like that when he sees it. My mother's Christmas tree was a sight to behold.

The second way my father compromised with my mother was that he let her sign his name on the little tags that were attached to the gifts we would have gotten anyway, which basically meant underwear and socks and T-shirts. We hated getting underwear and socks and T-shirts for Christmas. It seemed like such a cheat.

For us kids, the worst part about getting underwear and socks and T-shirts came later, on the first day back to school in January, when our mother made us wear our new clothes. Somehow we had it in our heads that only the poor kids got underwear and socks and T-shirts for Christmas, and that by wearing new clothes the first day back to school we were signaling to the world that we were poor. We begged our mother to let us wear old clothes, like the rich kids.

She never allowed that, but I think she understood our dilemma. Once when I was grown I asked her about that, and she said she included underwear and socks and T-shirts because that was the only way she could include my father's name on the cards as a giver of Christmas gifts. I think she hoped that we would think more kindly of my father and his convictions about Christmas gift giving. In an odd way, that was her gift to him.

The third way my father compromised with my mother had to do with something Mother called "the Snake Room."

I said that we lived in a three-story house, but that isn't quite the truth. Our house backed up against a hill, and the builder had built an entry directly out from the second floor onto the roadway that ran behind. That meant that the house had three stories on one side and two on the other. The builder hadn't excavated the slope of the hill but had left the slope as a kind of slanted crawl space. Where the slope of the hill intersected with the ground of the first floor he had built a wall, behind the platform where the pulpit had stood. In that wall was a small door.

My mother called the room behind the door "the Snake Room."

"Why?" I asked once, when I was maybe eight.

"Because that's where the snakes are," Mother said. "And spiders too. Huge spiders, some of them as big as your father's hand.

Tarantulas. Nasty things. Don't you ever go in the Snake Room."

"But what do the spiders and snakes eat in there?" I asked. "Do you feed them?"

"No," she said. "They eat each other. Awful mess. They eat little boys too."

"But we're all here, alive," I said. "Count us. We're all here. They haven't eaten any of *us*."

"They haven't eaten any that you know about, child," Mother said. "What if there were others who came before you? Never, ever go in the Snake Room."

I dropped the subject after that because it made my flesh crawl. I just didn't know for sure.

But I didn't stop thinking about it. One day, I think late in October, it got to be too much. I did what I had to do. After all, I was eight years old.

I went into the Snake Room.

It ruined Christmas for me that year.

The Snake Room was where my mother hid her Christmas presents. She had hundreds of presents in there. Boxes of them. Bags of them. Secreted away. Not organized so much as stashed. She bought Christmas presents all year long. After-Christmas sales. Year-end clearance sales. No sales at all.

My mother was a keen observer of her children's eyes, and whenever any little thing lit a spark in a child's eyes, Mother would go back later and add that something to her booty. She stashed it all in the Snake Room.

There's no lonelier feeling than the feeling that comes over you when you realize that, of all eight kids in the house, you're the only one who knows what the real Christmas presents are going to be, and you can't say a word to anybody. Then it dawns on you that on Christmas morning you're going to have to fake it. There's no lonelier moment than that.

So I went and got my little brother Joelie. Showed him. It took the edge off my guilt, and I knew that if I got in trouble I wouldn't be in trouble alone.

My father's compromise with the Snake Room came on Christmas Eve, after we kids had all gone to bed. Even though he disapproved of my mother's extravagant Christmas gift giving, he stayed up all night on Christmas Eve helping her wrap presents. They'd usually finish just as the sun was coming up, which meant that they were dropping into bed, exhausted, just as we were waking up. We would have to wait until later in the day for my parents to wake up before we could actually open anything, but they always let us at least sort our presents into piles while we waited. We rattled them and hefted them and pressed their sides. We sorted them and then sorted them again. We *prioritized* them. But we had to wait for our parents to get up before we could actually open them.

Mother would get up, fix herself a cup of coffee, and join us in the sanctuary. Then pandemonium would break loose.

Even now I can see my mother standing there in her bathrobe in the doorway, coffee cup in hand, watching us tear into the packages. She surveyed the room like this every year, drinking in the sights and sounds and smells of Christmas.

There was the twelve-foot Christmas tree, decorated with the ornaments of people she loved, all with stories to tell—the history of her family and friends. On the tree, the lights and the popcorn strings to remind us of the war years when everybody had to make do or do without, and her joy that her brothers had come home safe from the war.

There was the poinsettia on the stairs that Mr. Flory had given her to remind her that there were other romantics in the world.

There were the children, all eight of us, still in our pajamas but no longer sleepy—me and my sister and our brothers and our cousins, wearing cowboy boots with our pajamas, with holsters and silver cap guns and cowboy hats with the lanyard trim threaded into holes that had been punched along the rim. We rode stick horses with upholstered plastic heads. We lassoed the dogs and shot off our cap guns and generally made it impossible for our parents to go back to sleep.

There were the piles of shredded wrapping paper, paper she tried every year to salvage and save for the following year, but always in vain.

There were the two dogs—Sancho, our

collie pup, and Ferdinand, the little bull terrier—romping and playing with the wrapping like it was a kind of canine catnip.

In the background were the sounds of my mother's old record player, with Bing Crosby dreaming of a white Christmas or Gene Autry singing about Rudolph the Red-Nosed Reindeer.

And of course, through it all, there was the subtle, pervasive smell of pine needles.

Once I paused long enough to gaze at my mother as she drank in this reverie, and suddenly I realized that I was seeing her in a new light. This was what my mother was like when she was at her very best. As tiny as she was, standing there in the doorway, and in my heart too, my mother was eleven-foot-four.

It was a flash, a momentary vision, gone as quickly as it had come, but it left an impression so strong that even now when

I close my eyes it still comes back. She was eleven-foot-four because, in spite of all obstacles, and in the teeth of my father's objections, she had made this all possible.

4

Something happened to my family during the summer of 1962, something that shouldn't be part of a Christmas story, so I'm not going to tell you what it was.

But I will tell you this: it was decisive, it happened all at once, and it was irreversible. So far as my mother's world was concerned, it was catastrophic. In the space of half an hour after this event, my father was gone from our home forever.

Within a month, my older brother John was out of the house, living in his truck. My sister was already grown and gone. My uncle Big Nathan had left the navy, married my aunt Nadine, and taken our cousins—Small Nathan, Vickie, and Pudge—back to live with them.

My mother was suddenly on her own, a single mother trying to raise her three youngest sons—Jim, me, and Joelie. She had no education to speak of, not finishing grammar school because of the Depression and, after that, the war. She had never worked outside of the home, and she had no marketable job skills.

Within two months the house was gone.

My mother and we boys moved into a kind of shack that was provided for us as a courtesy by the real estate agent who sold our home. His name was Arnie Oakum, and if this story does nothing other than honor Mr. Oakum's memory, it will have achieved a noble purpose. Mr. Oakum rescued my mother. He provided us with a roof over our heads, and he gave my mother a small salary

while she trained for a job as a reception-
ist in his real estate office. Eventually she
became his office manager.

To be fair, the house he provided wasn't
a shack at all. It was small, cheaply con-
structed, and badly maintained, but it was
dry and warm, and when my mother got
finished with it, it was clean.

For us kids, it was all a great adventure.
We missed our father's reliable habits and
even his strong sense of conviction, but we
didn't at all miss the times he was inflexible, and we enjoyed watching our mother
in her strange new freedom. The fighting
had stopped, and the house was peaceful.
We found ourselves laughing freely, living
the life of romance my mother believed was
the sign of the good life.

Things weren't so clear for my mother,
however. Sometimes she was filled with
self-doubt. I can remember sitting up with

her late at night as she wondered out loud whether or not she had "done right by" my father. I didn't completely understand what this meant, but I knew she was in anguish and that there wasn't anything I could do about it. She never so much as looked at another man, not once.

The low point came for my mother on Christmas of that year, 1962. There was no money for a Christmas tree. Not for any tree at all, not even a six-foot tree like the ones my father had always written into his budget.

On the first Monday of December she got out one of the hammers my father had left behind, and she went out behind the house to where there was an old pile of lumber grown over with grass. She picked among the lumber until she found some boards with the nails still in them. She pulled these out with the hammer until she had a large handful, which she brought in her pocket back to the house.

She cleared a space on the wall in the living room and took down the large picture of Jesus, and we helped her move aside the sofa.

There, in the space on the wall, she nailed up a large triangle to serve as a two-dimensional Christmas tree.

She outlined the shape with strings of lights, big-bulbed, colored lights to form a triangle, and then a string or two of smaller, pinpoint white lights.

To the triangle she added popcorn strings, strings that even in two dimensions reminded her of the war years, when nobody had anything and everybody had to make do. One of the strings had cranberries, to remind her of her gratitude that all of her brothers had returned safe from the front.

Then she hung the ornaments. There wasn't much space, so she carefully chose which to hang and which to leave sleeping in their boxes for another year. She included one from each of her brothers and her sister, and one from each of us children. She hung pictures of our cousins—Nathan, Vickie, and Pudge. She paused a long time before she hung the ornaments from my sister and my brother, neither of whom would be with us this Christmas. At the top, just beneath the peak of the triangle, she hung a picture of my dad.

Then, on a nail eight or ten inches above the top of this two-dimensional Christmas tree, she slipped the brass ring of her mother's porcelain angel.

She paused a minute. Out of the box she took some red Christmas napkins, folded them into the shapes of poinsettias, and placed them around the base of the tree—a hopeful reminder, I think, that even in a situation like that, romance is still alive in the world.

She turned to Joelie and gave the signal. Joelie flipped the switch that turned on the lights, and then, all at once, magically, it was Christmas.

Then my mother sat down on the edge of the sofa and cried.

It was the first time I ever saw my mother cry. Even now I don't know exactly why she cried.

Maybe she cried because she knew that we would never again have another twelve-foot Christmas tree like the ones we'd had in the past.

Maybe she cried because she missed my brother and my sister and my cousins and my dad. Whatever had transpired between them, my mother loved my father until the day she died. Would it be as hard for him this Christmas, missing her, as it was now for her, missing him?

Maybe she cried because she knew that all

she would have to put under this little two-dimensional Christmas tree would be the things we would have gotten anyway—underwear and socks and T-shirts.

I sat down beside her on the sofa, right there in the middle of the living room, and I put my arm around her, and she rested her head on my shoulder. She turned her tiny face up to mine, my mother did, and she said that in all her life she had never felt so small.

That was when my brothers and I decided that this would never happen to our mother again.

5

The following year, late in October and then into November, we began to save our money. This was really hard to do because we were just three boys—me, my older brother Jim, and youngest of all, Joelie. We didn't get any allowance since my mother couldn't afford it. We made our money every which way we could.

We washed the neighbor's car for fifty cents. One time. We put the fifty cents in a mason jar that we kept behind the books on the shelf above Jim's bed.

We walked old ladies to their cars at Bud Cavender's market up the road, hoping for a nickel or a dime for a tip. That worked out pretty well until Mr. Cavender came out and chased us away with a meat cleaver. I don't think he meant to threaten us with the meat cleaver—it was just what he happened to have in his hand at the time—but it looked menacing enough there in his hand, so we never went back after that.

Mr. Flory gave us a quarter each for helping him put up the Christmas tree lot beside his peanut stand. By my father's definition, this made us pagans like Mr. Flory was, but we fell back on our mother's opinion that what mattered was that we came by the money honestly.

Most of our money came from collecting soda bottles around the empty lots near our house—Coca-Cola and Pepsi and Grape Nehi—and turning them in for their California redemption value, which at that time was three cents a bottle. Very gradually, too gradually, the little mason jar began to fill. We checked it every night. Sometimes it seemed like we were racing a clock. I had never experienced a deadline before, and this one was terrible.

On the first Monday of December, when we got home from school, we went for the tree.

We poured the money out on my brother's bed and counted it up: $4.57 in change. Four dollars and fifty-seven cents. Not much by today's standards. It wasn't much in December of 1963 either, but it was all we had, and it was honest money, legally earned, even if some of it had come from the pagan enterprise of helping Mr. Flory set up the Christmas tree lot next to his peanut stand.

Jim put the money in his jacket pocket, and we trooped down to Ollie Flory's Christmas tree lot.

We found the only tree in the lot that could be had for $4.57. It was barely three feet tall and was so thin Mr. Flory hadn't nailed one of those crosspieces on the bottom for fear the trunk would split. He told us he had saved it for us, and we found it lying flat on its side behind his truck.

It had uneven branches, with a dense, thick place down on the right side and almost nothing on the left half near the top. What branches it did have were clustered all on one side, which was another reason Mr. Flory hadn't made a crosspiece base for it. It would have fallen over from the imbalance of its weight.

Looking back now, I realize that Mr. Flory could have given us the tree, but he was wise enough to know that that would have made it his gift, not ours. He didn't need to sell it; we needed to buy it. He did give us a poinsettia plant as a courtesy, he said, in memory of the old days. Mr. Flory wasn't a pagan; he was a romantic.

We carried the tree and the poinsettia home triumphantly, the three of us, trading the weight between us and making a plan as we went.

Jim and I moved the sofa in the living room and cleared a place against the wall. We took down the picture of Jesus. Jim tied a string to the tree and hung it from the picture nail.

Joelie went in the kitchen and popped popcorn and made popcorn strings. He found cranberries in a bag in the freezer, and some of these he interspersed between the popcorn on one of the strings.

We hung a string of those big-bulbed lights, the kind that spread a soft glow around. Most of the lights ended up on the lower right part of the tree where the densest branches were, but Jim put a couple of nails in the wall to help out the thinner part on the upper left.

We added a string of the pinpoint lights—just one string, because we were afraid of making the tree too heavy for the nail in the wall, and because we had to save room for the ornaments and for Joelie's popcorn strings.

The ornaments were a problem because there were so many, but Jim said he had to make something called an "executive decision," which was an expression I didn't fully understand. Then he selected out of the box one store-bought ornament for each of my mother's brothers and one for her sister. For each of the kids he added one of those Sunday school ornaments with our pictures on them. There was a photograph of Joelie, ringed in Cheerios, and a paper plate angel of me, and another of Jim. He added ornaments that had been made by our cousins—Nathan, Vickie, and Pudge.

Pride of place went to the ornaments for my brother and my sister, neither of whom would be with us this Christmas. Somewhere near the top he hung a photograph of our dad.

Then came the popcorn strings, one of them laced with cranberries, to remember the war years, when people had to make do or do without, and to remind my mother of her relief and delight when her brothers came home safe from the front.

Finally, the *coup de grâce*—my grandmother's porcelain Christmas angel. We added a nail eight or ten inches above the peak of the tree and hung the angel by the brass ring between her shoulder blades.

We set out the poinsettia plant Mr. Flory had given us; then we went into the kitchen to wait.

It was dark when my mother got home. Winter nights came early to our part of the country. We saw the headlights of her car turn into the drive and then held our breath as the tires crunched to a halt on the gravel driveway outside.

She came in by the back door, into the kitchen. She hesitated there at the door as if she wasn't quite sure what was happening. I could see that she sensed there was something different in the house.

Perhaps it was Joelie's Cheshire-cat grin.

Maybe it was the tiny bits of popcorn that we had forgotten to sweep up after making the popcorn strings.

Maybe it was the fact that we were all sitting there in the dark because we had been so excited we forgot to turn on the lights.

I think it was the smell of the pine needles.

Without a word, Mother followed her senses down the hall into the living room.

Just as she stepped into the living room, Joelie slipped past her; his fingers found the switch that turned on the strings of lights, and then, all at once, magically, it was Christmas.

That was the second time I ever saw my mother cry.

I like to think that she cried because she realized that even though we would never see another twelve-foot Christmas tree, it didn't really matter. Everything would be alright.

Mother's gone now, and I'll never be able to ask her why she cried that night. But I can tell you why I cried. I cried because all at once I realized that both my mother and my father had been right after all. It all had to do with the meaning of gift giving.

My father had said there was nothing at all about Christmas presents that could be reduced to a business transaction. No giving in order to get, no earning gifts by being good enough, no obligation, no payment for services rendered. It wasn't a matter of deserving what you got, of being good enough, of merit. It wasn't that my mother did or didn't deserve this gift from us three boys. It was that the question of deserving this gift never entered our heads. We didn't give her this gift because of who she was, either. We did it because of who she was *to us.*

My mother had said that the inner freedom to do something absolutely extravagant was the closest human beings ever come to feeling what God must feel when he is being gracious toward us, that when we give an extravagant gift we somehow rise above ourselves and become a little better than we were. "A little larger on the inside," my mother had said.

My mother looked across at us three boys—all of us in tears. She stood up straight. Without a word, all four of us drew ourselves up to our full heights, and for the first time in my life I knew what it was like to be eleven-foot-four.

That's the way it happened, the Christmas of 1963, the Christmas that I learned the meaning of grace.

Joseph's Son

*S*hhh. Hush now. You'll wake your mother."

The workman had heard women in the village describe babies as helpless, and maybe that was true for most babies, but it wouldn't be for any baby born in *his* house. This one had a lusty squall that seemed to match the storm swirling outside—which he felt had come inside too, and his heart was troubled by it because he didn't know what to do. There were other storms on the horizon for his little family, just as there were people everywhere; people and pack animals swirled about them, and he was grateful that the innkeeper and his wife had moved on and left them alone at last. That part of their personal storm had subsided, at least for a while.

Two of the women in the inn had joined them to help as best they could, and he had been dismissed with the innkeeper to bring water and bedding and old clothes. "This is women's work," they'd said, but they were gone now too, off to tend to the needs of their own families, and the stable was quiet once again.

"Your mother is sleeping now, boy," said the workman. "And after the struggle of this long night, it's a wonder you can sleep at all. Mary's sleep I can understand. This has been a long journey. The donkey . . . the desperation to find a place . . . the strangers for midwives." The women had been pressed into service by circumstance, not because they knew the arts of midwifing, but merely because they were women and had happened to be close at hand.

And so the birth had been hard—the whole thing had been hard—but it was over now, and at last it was just the three of them. The workman. His wife. Their first child, a son.

"Shhh," he whispered again to the baby. "Shhh. Your mother's sleeping now, boy. Let's not wake her up. She's had a long journey, and it's going to be even longer before it's finished."

The baby calmed a little and looked up at him, not making eye contact. Maybe it was too soon to hope for eye contact, but the child was clearly aware of the workman's presence. Whatever went on in the mind of an infant, the workman wasn't quite sure. The child's mother might know, but she was sleeping, and who could blame her? She was exhausted by the journey, by the crowds, by the birth itself with the aftermath of bustling women, by the cleaning up, and then by that odd thing with the shepherds.

He pulled the heavy saddle blanket closer

around his shoulders and hunkered more deeply into the straw that the innkeeper had banked up along one side of the stable, then rolled over slowly and gazed at his wife in the darkness. He reached out and smoothed a stray lock from her forehead.

All of it had been too much for her. And how old was she now? She was barely out of childhood herself. It wasn't any wonder she'd fallen into a deep slumber, but the baby was crying again and Joseph didn't want to wake her, not after what she'd been through.

Maybe gentle rocking would settle the baby, and Mary could get some more sleep. Even as the workman thought this, he hesitated. The thought of touching the baby made him self-conscious, and he found himself oddly shy in the presence of his own son.

What gave him pause was a sudden, strange awareness of his hands.

They were rough hands, a workman's hands, and Joseph was afraid that maybe the baby would cry again if he touched him, brushed against him. His own mother had told him once that the tenderness needed for holding babies was a tenderness of the heart, and that even callused hands would serve just fine if the heart was soft enough, but still he hesitated.

He reached down and gently disentangled the baby from Mary's sleeping grasp, lifting him out and up, then settling him down where he could lay his small head on the workman's shoulder. He took care not to rustle Mary's bedding. Very slowly he shook out the wrinkles in the blanket, holding the baby out just a little so the blanket could fall free. Then he settled back little by little into the deep pile of straw. The child was so small, and lusty squall or not, all of a sudden he seemed so tiny there. Joseph thought for a moment that he could cradle the baby in a single one of his callused hands.

"Workmen like me do our thinking with our hands," he said at last. "Your mother would be shocked to hear me going on like this." But then he said, "Still, sometimes it helps to set your thoughts out on the table, to take their measure, test their seams, and see if they're properly joined and nicely finished."

He hummed a little tune, turning his face until the ends of his beard brushed the feather-fine hair on the top of the baby's head, and it occurred to him that this must be the softest, gentlest feeling a man can have—to have the tips of his beard brush the head of his own newborn child.

The baby pushed hard against his chest and turned to him and yawned and made eye contact, and then, exhausted by this effort, settled down on Joseph's shoulder once again and looked at him out of one eye. Then he leaned in deep and closed both eyes.

When the baby opened his tiny mouth and slipped in an even tinier thumb, the workman found his heartbeat adjusting to the gentle rhythm of thumb-sucking. "There," he said, "settle down."

There was another long pause.

"Shhh," he said again. "It's a terrible thing that we've come to this. Children of kings, after all, child. Did you know that?" The baby opened one eye. "You're descended from the most famous king of all. Descended from David, you are. Did you know that? And we've been reduced to this. Strangers alone in a foreign town. . . . It's a terrible thing.

"These are your people, boy. You've come to your own, but then your own didn't receive you."

The baby yawned again and sucked his

thumb, as if he couldn't care less that his own had not received him. He was here, he was alive, and that in itself was a miracle of God. The workman hesitated; perhaps he had been too harsh in what he'd said. As cold as it was outside, it might be better here in the stable after all, away from the noise and hubbub of the inn. He gazed around the room, looking hard in the dim light, listening to the lowing of the cattle, tracing the outline of his own donkey in the corner stall.

Mary stirred and looked at him but said nothing.

He held the baby up for her to see. "Woman," he said, smiling, "behold your son."

She smiled back, sighed, and slipped again into the sweet oblivion of sleep.

A biting wind slipped through a knife-thin crack in the stable wall. The workman muttered something strong under his breath and instinctively wished he had brought his toolbox, but then he remembered the night and the sleeping baby and his wife. He stood and held the baby close with one hand and went to the wall, quietly moving a loose board into place to cut off the wind. He moved slowly, stepping carefully across the dirt floor, barely able to see in the dim light of the oil lamp the innkeeper had left them.

"Shhh. He's a good man," the workman whispered, as though such a comment could dispel any lingering questions the baby might have about the innkeeper's character. "He's got to see to his guests, that's all. How would it be if they came to his inn and in the room next door there was a woman giving birth? Or a squalling newborn?" He swatted a fly away with his free hand, then settled back into the straw.

"Your mother has such visions for you.

'He'll be a king,' she says, and I believe it, at least in part. The seed of David, after all. She tells me of an angel. I've never understood talk about visions. I have only dreams, never visions."

He drifted off for a moment, and the lamplight dimmed. "Well, isn't this a divine comedy? So where are your heralds? The visiting viziers? The heads of state to welcome your birth?"

The baby sighed then, and the lamp nearly flickered out. The innkeeper had given them only enough oil to see them off to sleep, and even though the workman was nearly delirious from exhaustion, he couldn't rest just now because he would have no way to relight the lamp in the dark if it should go out completely. He thought of how tiny the light was in the stable and how quickly they would run out of oil, and he hoped that his wife wouldn't need him in the pitch dark.

"Some birth for a king!" he said as he rocked forward to stand up. He still held the sleeping child, managing to add the remaining oil to the lamp with his free hand. He paused there for a moment, holding the light, and he thought about other kinds of darkness that had crept into the world.

"Some birth for a king," he muttered again under his breath. But then he thought, *This boy will be a workman. A king? Maybe so. The seed of David, after all. But a workman, surely, whatever else he will be. There may be kingdom enough in a carpenter's shop.*

He eased the child down to a cradling position in the crook of his right arm. Then he rose and went to the pail of warm milk the midwives had left. He found a cloth, twisted the end into a point, and dipped it in the pail, shaking off the excess as carefully as he could, then used the tip of his smallest finger to remove the baby's thumb from his mouth, replacing it with the point. The sucking increased, intensified by a satisfied murmur.

The workman hummed, then stopped again to speak to the baby, keeping his voice so low he almost didn't hear it himself above the sound of the sucking: "King or not, any child of my house will be a craftsman too. No shame in that. My own father used to say as much to me: 'Remember, boy, you are descended from kings. Let your work be worthy of a king, even if your scepter is a saw and your throne a carpenter's bench. Let your work be worthy of a king. Remember your father David, boy. A shepherd as well as a king. No shame in working with your hands, boy. Just as the king was already there in the shepherd, so was the shepherd always there in the king.'"

The workman refreshed the cloth, shook the excess milk, and replaced it gently in the baby's mouth. In his mind's eye he caught a glimpse of this boy grown up, the king his mother dreamed of. He wondered where this baby would find the wine tasters to sit with him at the head table and drink from the cup that he would drink. "You'll need advisers to sit with you beside your throne."

Joseph rocked and hummed and wondered what sort of people would shape the policies of this baby's kingdom if Mary should be right. "Where does a king with calluses turn for advice?" he whispered. "Who will be your advisers? I can see it now, boy. You'll have one on your right hand, the other on your left. But who? Day laborers? Maybe shepherds, maybe fishermen. People of the land, every one. Will they be common people, like your father?" *A king could do worse than take the advice of a common man,* he thought. *The ones who rule everything right now—what do they know?* "Show me a man who lays stone for a living, and I'll show you a man with practical wisdom, a man who will find a way to get the hard jobs done." He paused again. He repeated the ablutions with the milk and the cloth. "Be kind to them," he murmured, as though the baby would understand. He was wondering where the thought had come from, when it was followed by another, equally puzzling: "Forgive them. They won't know what they're doing."

The workman shifted the baby back to his shoulder, gave him a gentle thumping on the back. The baby burped a little and then wriggled and moved his head deeper into the fold of the workman's chin. Satisfied with the feeding, he returned to his thumb, reaching up instinctively with his free hand and clasping the workman's earlobe.

He patted the baby softly then, for the

moment taken up by the realization that this was a hard job too.

"Are you alright in there?" It was the voice of one of the workers at the inn, sent to check on them in the storm.

Joseph rose, still holding the child, and went to the door, opening it slightly to whisper to the questioner outside. It seemed to creak more loudly in the dark than it had in the light. "All is calm, all is bright," he whispered, and turned back to the bed in the straw. But it wasn't bright. It was dark, very dark, and getting darker as the storm lashed the shutters.

He distracted himself from his worry by continuing to talk to the child. "Think kindly of the common people, the people like that fellow out there, come out on a stormy night to check on you. Their daily bread is hard-earned. Listen to them. The people who work the land have their stories to tell too.

And they're proud to work, most of them. A man's work is the signature he signs on his life. There's no shame in working with your hands, boy. Remember that you come from worthy people—not just David, a flawed man but God's man too. In your veins runs the blood of a thousand nameless ancestors, every one as noble as David."

Mary's breathing paused from its normal rhythm. He waited, then slowly rose until he was standing straight up in the darkness. He didn't walk but stood there swaying, holding the baby against his chest, humming a little tune he'd heard somewhere, a deep-throated tune, so the baby would be comforted by the resonating chest wall and by the beating of his father's soft heart.

"Blessed quietness, holy quietness. . . ."

He paused. "Shhh." The baby had resumed his thumb-sucking, his quiet drift

back to sleep marked by an almost mystical stillness in the room.

Three or four of the hens were startled awake by the barking of a dog close by. The baby, still sleeping, responded to the burst of cackling by sucking harder on his thumb, then settled down again to the rhythm of the gentle cooing as the hens went back to sleep.

"Shhh," the workman said again. He returned to the song:

"Blessed quietness, holy quietness,
What assurance in my soul. . . ."

Off in the distance the wind picked up and a door flapped open, slapping hard against the wall of some building he could not remember having seen. A flash of lightning, and then after a pause, a crack of thunder, and then after that, a sudden downpour. The workman thought of the many, many storms his little family would face in the uncertain times that lay ahead. A rising and falling wind gave the downpour a thrumming quality against the outside walls, which oddly calmed the child and, in turn, reassured the workman. He wondered if the child would be able to sleep in that *other* kind of storm.

He finished what he knew of the song:

"On the stormy sea, he speaks peace to me;
How the billows cease to roll."

When the last of the oil was gone, the lamp went out and the workman was plunged into near total darkness. His ears took over then, and his fingertips. Suddenly feeling small in the darkness, he listened and felt his way and was painfully aware of his fingers as they walked along the edges of his wife's blanket. They were big, rawboned fingers, callused like the palms of his hands, and scarred from accidents in the shop when he was younger and still learning his trade, but they were skilled fingers now too. They felt rather than groped in the dark. Then he stopped and whispered again in the quiet: "Remember this, some night when you're old, and your mother's visions have become an old man's memories. . . . One night, a man older than you once told you this: a man's character is marked by what he does with his hands. Be careful where your calluses come from . . . and the scars on your hands. Your mother dreams that you will be king, and I dream of a king with calluses."

He listened for the gentle rhythm of Mary's breathing and heard her sigh and turn a little, rustling the straw as she nestled in more deeply against the cold.

The baby cried out, startled at something. Did infants dream?

"Shhh," he said. "You're dreaming. Let's

not wake your mother." The workman suddenly felt imbalanced in the dark, so he settled back into the straw once again, taking care not to wake Mary or disturb the sleeping child.

"And if you do become king," he said, "build for David a strong house, a strong kingdom. With well-hung doors. And square corners. And heavy crossbeams. Many a king could learn from a carpenter, I tell you. . . . Work slowly. Do not hurry the work. Be humble. Before you complain about the dust in your brother's eye, check for splinters in your own. Remember the common people, the people whose scepters are only saws and whose thrones are only workbenches. They too may be noble, sons of a king. They too are children of Abraham, after all."

He thought of the legacy of a kingdom, reduced to the carpenter's bench, and wondered if that was something the boy would

remember too. "Remember the feel of the saw in your hands . . . and the weight of the nails . . . and the heft of the timbers. . . . Whatever kingdom comes to you, may you be a king with calluses.

"So as I hold you now this night, I offer you this blessing:

> "Whatever kingdom comes to you,
>   child,
> May you never forget
> The weight of the crossbeams on
>   your shoulders
> And the feel of the carpenter's nails
>   in your hands."

Through a Glass Darkly

For now we see in a mirror dimly, but then face to face. Now I know in part; then I shall understand fully, even as I have been fully understood.

1 Corinthians 13:12

The face is the mirror of the soul; the eyes tell, without speaking, the secrets of the heart.

St. Jerome

*T*he stinking worst thing about Christmas is the cleanup.

Last year Angie had been left alone to clean up the mess and put all the Christmas decoration junk away, drag the stupid Christmas tree outside and cut it down to size so she could stuff it in the car and haul it out to the killing fields the town fathers had taken over by eminent domain and turned into a dump. The dump was named after Angie's uncle Joey, who used to be the manager before he retired. Angie thought that was perfect because Joey still smelled like the dump, and he was too dense to see the superb irony of having a town dump named after him. It was called the Joseph McCracken Refuse Facility, and since Angie was family they let her unload the tree for free. Big deal. There wasn't another girl in the county who had family privileges at the stinking town dump.

When she pulled up, a big, coarse-cut man in dirty engineer's overalls jerked the tree out of her trunk and tossed it up onto the bonfire without a word, then walked away to a battered Chevy truck that was pulling up. As she watched the tree go up in smoke she thought of the Bonfire of

the Vanities and pretended she was somewhere else.

After that, the trunk of her car smelled
like Pine-Sol for-like-*ever*, and dried pine
needles kept popping up between the seat
cushions for months and months, sticking
her in the armpits and snagging her only
sweater. It was summer before the last of
the sap finally worked its way out of the
carpet in her trunk by sticking itself to the
bottom of the only good backpack she had
ever owned.

This year it was the same thing all over
again. Her mother had gone to work, which
left her and her sister Joanna to clean up,
but Joanna had left too because that party-
animal boyfriend of hers had pulled up in
the Chevy truck his father bought him and
honked, and Joanna had run off and left
Angie to clean up everybody else's mess by
herself. She started taking off the ornaments

while the breakfast dishes were still piled high in the kitchen next to the pots and pans from last night's supper—she would have to wash those too.

She looked around at the mess, letting the messiness of it work its way into her bones. She *felt* like this room *looked*. Packed down into the corners of the couch were tiny bits of that sticky-sweet Christmas popcorn her sister's boyfriend had dropped. He had been considerate enough to work the popcorn into the fabric of the couch with his rear end.

On the wall above the couch hung a garage sale picture frame with a single black-and-white photograph of her father, whom she flatly called "John," because she had no memory of him and thought it sounded stupid to use words like "Father" and "Daddy" for a perfect stranger. His real name was Arthur, but she called him "John" anyway—short for "John Doe." Her father had skipped out on them just ten months after Joanna was born. They were better off without him. He was a deadbeat. Arthur McCracken—John Doe. A nobody. Maybe a drifter. If John Doe ever came around her or her mother again, she'd beat him out of the house with a stick.

She had no idea why her mother had nailed his picture up on the wall above the sofa. The way Angie saw it, hanging the picture was a waste of a good nail.

She started with the tree, stripping off the ornaments a dozen at a time, hanging them on the fingers of her right hand and making little trips to the kitchen, where she laid them on the counter next to the dirty dishes.

She had cleared off the last of the ornaments and begun unstringing the lights when she noticed something down behind the tree—another gift maybe, the size of a small book, wrapped in what looked like reused paper and a badly crumpled ribbon. She picked it up. Turned it over. It looked like it had been opened and repackaged a dozen times already. Whoever had done that had even reused the old tape so it no longer held, and one of the corners was torn off completely, and the exposed corner showed a plain cardboard box.

On the back, slapped on with tape, was a handwritten tag that said "McCracken." She shook the box. Hard object inside, heavier on one end. She tried to figure what it was from the way it shifted oddly in the box.

McCracken. That could be anybody. Could be her. Could be Joanna. Her mother, maybe. Maybe even John Doe, but only if somebody had made a stupid mistake.

How did it get here? Nobody in the family would have written "McCracken." Her mother would have written "Angie" or "Jo-anna," or maybe both their names. She took it to the couch, rattled it, set it on the coffee table. Went to the kitchen. Poured a cup of stale black coffee, brought it back to sip as she inspected the package. She didn't recognize the handwriting on the tag, and there was no clue about how it had ended up under their tree.

It didn't take all that long to decide she would open it up and see what it was. If she needed to, she would rewrap it and nobody would know.

It was a mirror. Polished silver. A hand mirror, with a deep engraving of a girl in a Roman tunic on the handle. It was not like any mirror she had ever seen. She took it to the window to get better light. Held it up. Looked at it again, and nearly fainted. In the oval frame of the mirror, she saw the Christmas tree behind her, but its lights were on and glowing, and the ornaments were back in place. She turned around and looked. The tree was bare. She held the mirror up again, this time angling so she could see the tree and its reflection at the same time. The one was bare; the other was covered by softly glowing lights.

She made a slow rotation around the room, checking everything in the oblique angle of the glass. Everything looked new—in the mirror. On the wall above the couch, where the black-and-white photo of John Doe had hung, there was an oil painting of a man she did not recognize. The face in the painting was smiling—a warm, friendly face. The man was seated. He wore a green, double-breasted suit, new but cut in a way that would have been in style maybe fifteen or twenty years ago. *That couldn't be John,* she thought.

She lowered the mirror and looked around

the room again. Bare, dry tree. Black-and-white photograph of John on the wall. She knelt on the couch and held the mirror close to the photograph, its edge touching the wall and the glass at an angle so she could see the photograph and the reflection at the same time. The man in the photograph was John, but—it took a moment to think this through—the man she saw in the mirror was her father, Arthur.

She went into the bathroom and pulled the chain on the bare bulb that hung over the sink, then looked at herself in the bathroom mirror. The hard light made her look the way she felt—angular and ugly, at odds with the world. Angie had a look that grown-ups had often described as *sullen*. She had a sallow complexion with permanent zits that surrounded an open, unhealed sore on her right cheek. Her hair was straight, thin, almost wispy, and she often caught herself absentmindedly fingering it or pulling it down to chew the ends with her teeth. Her mother had called her stupid for that because the oil in her hair had only made the open sore on her cheek that much worse.

In the harsh light of the bulb above the mirror, she could see the hardness in her eyes, the don't-touch-me-or-I'll-take-you-down look, which was why the grown-ups called her sullen. If anybody had a right to be sullen, she did. It was her posture of defiance against an unfair world. *What comes around goes around,* she thought. This is what the world had given her, so this was what she would give back. Being sullen was a badge she wore—not proudly, but defiantly.

She held up the oval mirror she had taken from the box. Even in the hard light of the bare bathroom bulb, the image in the mirror was her, but not her. Her hair, still black, was brushed and clean. It had been put up in a

French braid by somebody, but she didn't know who. Her mother didn't know how to make a French braid. The face in the hand mirror was softer than the face she saw in the mirror above the sink. The skin was healed. The sullen look was gone. She closed her eyes so she couldn't see either image, then reached up and touched her face. She winced when her fingers touched the raw sore on her cheek. She looked at herself in the hand mirror. The face had skin like a baby. She brushed her hair with the tips of her fingers, and the image repeated the gesture exactly. She touched the sore again, and while she felt the sore beneath the tips of her fingers, in the mirror the skin was clear.

How all this happened she did not know, but the mirror was mocking her with her own face, and for a moment she thought about throwing it in the bathroom trash or taking it out back and smashing it with a rock. Instead she held it up and glared at it, making the hard, sullen look her mother hated; the reflection in the mirror smiled back. She hated that. The smile was insipid, stupid. The face in the mirror pitied her, or it was mocking her—she didn't know which. She looked again, and the face had softened again into a clean, steady gaze, inspecting her as she inspected it. She held the mirror out at arm's length, and the gaze grew steadier, softer, gentler, and she realized that the look she was seeing wasn't pity but compassion. She hated that too.

She looked back and forth between the girl in the hand mirror and the truer picture of herself in the bathroom mirror. Her real self wore jeans and an old T-shirt. The girl in the mirror wore a beautiful, off-white antique lace dress, with a carved ivory cameo brooch at the throat. The cameo was exquisite—the girl in the bas-relief profile wore a French braid that duplicated the braid worn by the girl in the mirror. In tiny, reversed mirror-image letters around the outside top edge of the cameo, an inscription read, "Angela." Tiny numbers inscribed on the bottom edge gave her birthday.

When she saw the name and face on the cameo, she sat down on the toilet and cried.

She didn't put the mirror back in the box, and she decided not to tell anybody about it either. Instead she wrapped it in an old T-shirt and stashed it in her backpack, then went back to the sorry task of cleaning up her family's Christmas mess.

She hauled the tree outside. Old Lady Keillor, the crazy who lived next door, was wandering outside in her nightgown, shivering with cold, talking to an invisible companion. She wore white elbow-length gloves and a mink stole but no coat, and Angie could see the old woman's breath around her head like the cloud over Everest. Angie went to the fence and told the old crone to go inside or she'd freeze, that there was nobody there.

She went into the garage, found a rusty saw her father had left behind, went back to the tree, and cut off the larger branches so she could stuff it into the trunk of her car. She stuck the loose branches into the backseat and headed out to her uncle's dump.

There was nobody around, just that same hard guy who had been here the year before. He might be an old drunk, but if he was, she figured he was a reliable old drunk. He probably lived out there in the dump, maybe in one of the junk cars that ringed the dump like a fence. She never saw him anywhere else, just here. He looked like a garden gone to seed. His hair was a wild tangle of gray. He must have had only the one pair of coveralls. When she pulled up to the bonfire, he jerked her tree out of the trunk with one hand—whatever else, he was strong—then shouted at her that she'd pulled her car too close to the fire and she should get the heck out of there. She bit her lip to keep from giving him back what he had given her. It felt like the spirit of Christmas was going up in the smoke of the bonfire.

She pulled the car a little farther out, parking where she could see the old guy in the rearview mirror. She reached into her backpack, took out the oval hand mirror, and held it up so she could see the old man's reflection. He continued to work there, taking dry Christmas trees out of the trunks of cars that had lined up alongside the edge of the dump, but in the mirror he was younger by maybe twenty years. His hair was dark, neatly combed, wavy. He was wearing a dark suit and tie. Even his shoes showed shiny in the glistening light of the bonfire. And he wasn't alone. There was a young girl, maybe five years old. The man watched over the girl as he worked, keeping her out of the flow of cars, watching that she didn't get too close to the fire. Sometimes he picked her up and held her in the crook of one arm as he worked the trees with the other. Once when there was a lull in the line, he hoisted her up on his shoulders and smiled while she played with his hair. As Angie watched, the child reached down and cupped her hands around the old man's ears against the cold. When she did that, he pulled her down and tickled her hard in the stomach.

What was this, anyway? Angie looked again without the mirror. From time to time, the old man reached out to touch a presence that was not there, the missing presence of the child. It was a clue, a kind of puzzle she would have to work out for herself. The habituated gestures into thin air were the gestures of a father reaching for a daughter who wasn't there. In the absence of the child, the father wasn't gruff or angry, as she had thought, but awkward and lonely. The gruffness was the voice of a broken heart.

She reached into her backpack and pulled out a candy bar, got out of the car, and went over to where the man was working.

She held out the candy bar. He waved her off. "Get outta the way, got a truck pulling up."

She stepped aside then and let him work, but stayed anyway and watched him. Up close, too, he had that same body language, the tiny, empty gestures into thin air, the glances backward and around to make sure the little girl was safe. When the next vehicle pulled up, she stepped in beside him and helped him wrench the Christmas tree from the trunk, then stepped back as he tossed it on the bonfire. It didn't take more than two or three cars before they had a rhythm going. She took the top, the old man took the bottom. She said, "One, two, three, pull," and they yanked together, then she stepped out of the way while he tossed the tree up onto the bonfire and another vehicle pulled up to the now-empty spot.

They had worked that way for more than an hour before there was anything like a lull. When the last of the cars had pulled away, he sat down on a large rock and looked at her.

"Still got that candy bar?"

She sat down beside him. Pulled the candy from her pocket. A crumbling chocolate mess, hard from the cold but still sweet. She handed him half.

"What'd you say your name was?" he asked.

"Angela," she said. "Angie. My friends call me Angie."

Another car pulled up. After this, they talked a little as they worked. Short sentences. Sentence fragments, punctuated by hard breathing and the slap of the branches against the sides and backs of cars. "Look out, there."

"Sorry."

More than once, he said something like, "I know that family. Got a place out on the ridge route. Kid went bad." He asked about her family. She told him about her mother. Gave him an earful about Joanna leaving her to clean up. More than once he stood beside her and rested his hand lightly on her shoulder, or touched her arm as she passed beside him. They could have been two co-workers anywhere, sharing the work, sharing the moments of rest. They could have been a father with his child.

She had to peel off when the sun went down, but just before she left him, she stopped cold in her work, looked him in the eye, and asked about the girl. She didn't know how else to raise the question but to be direct: "What's her name?"

"Whose name?"

"You had a child once, didn't you? A daughter maybe. What's her name?"

"*Was*," he said flatly. He looked away. "What *was* her name."

She stood with her back to the bonfire, and she watched as his gaze drifted behind her and was swallowed in the flames. There was a long silence. Finally, he said, "Doesn't matter now."

A final car pulled up, and she and the old man went out to clear its tree and finish up their work. Something had happened to the old man's daughter, and she didn't know what it was, but she knew she wouldn't ask. It was clearly painful. He would tell her what he wanted her to know. Probably not more than that. It was none of her business anyway.

She went to her car. He let her go without a word, without saying thanks, and she had the odd sense that somehow thanks would have been inappropriate. If there were reason for thanks, it was something she owed the mirror. Somehow it had helped her see the old man differently, to see him as his better self, the younger self who had a tender connection with a daughter now gone. Somehow it had asked her to treat him more kindly because of his loss.

"Where've you been?" her mother asked when she got home. Her mother was still wearing her waitress dress from work, with

splatters of spaghetti sauce and the name
badge with "Marian" stuck on in label-gun
tape that had long since been rubbed so
flat nobody could have made it out. Didn't
matter anyway. They lived in a small town.

"Out at the dump," Angie said. "There's
an old guy works out there all alone, burn-
ing the Christmas trees."

As they talked, Angie could hardly help
but wonder what had happened to the old
man's little girl. The memory was so painful he couldn't say her name out loud. She
thought of her own father and wondered
what had happened to take him from her.

"Mother," she said. "What really happened
to . . ." She hesitated, thought *John*, thought
better of that, and finally finished the question with, "Daddy?"

"Arthur?" her mother asked, apparently
unsure of where this line of reasoning was
taking them. The water on the stove was

boiling now, and she poured in a box of macaroni.

"Was there another woman?"

"It's not what you think," her mother said.

"How do you know what I think?"

Her mother ignored the implied barb in the question. "There was an accident at the plant," she said.

"What plant?" Angie asked.

"Newspaper. Your father was a pressman. One of the rollers on the biggest press broke loose, and half the crew got hurt. Your father wasn't the only one, but he got hurt the worst."

"I didn't know that," Angie said, realizing that perhaps she had not known him well enough to hate him as deeply as she did. She stood, went to a drawer, and took out silverware. Got plates. Took them to the table.

"Your father's a proud man," her mother went on. "His left hand got crushed beneath the roller. He lost three fingers."

"Which meant he couldn't work," Angie realized.

"Not as a pressman," her mother agreed. "I had to take over, get the job at the diner, and your father stayed home, trying to take care of you and Joanna. He was no good at that. Spent every day on the couch there. I think he was in a lot of pain."

"Did he ever get well enough to go back to work?" Angie asked.

"After a while, the morphine didn't do any more good," her mother said, "and when the insurance money ran out, there wasn't even that, and your father would groan and rub his hand for hours. He drank some, to cut the ache in his hand. And his heart. I think the real pain was in his shame that I was the one putting the bread on the table, which he thought was the man's work."

"But the accident wasn't his fault," Angie pointed out.

Her mother shook her head. "Didn't matter. When the press took his hand, it took his self-respect."

"Didn't you tell him?" Angie said.

"Everybody tried to tell him," her mother said. "Your father'd always been proud. He heard what he wanted to hear." She drained the macaroni through a colander and mixed in the cheese, got a hot pad, and set the pan on the table. Angie ran water from the faucet into glasses and brought them to the table, and the two women sat there in silence for a moment—the closest their family could come to saying grace. "All the talk in the world couldn't give him back his hand," her mother said. There was a long pause. "Or his self-respect."

"Why'd he leave us, then?" Angie spooned the hot macaroni onto her plate. She set down the pan and looked at her mother, waiting.

"I went to work one day, and when I got back there was a note that you and your sister were next door with Mrs. Keillor." Long silence. "The note said he was sorry, but that it'd be easier on me if I didn't have to feed an invalid too. God, I loved that man."

"I hate him," Angie said.

"You haven't lived long enough to be your father's judge," said her mother.

Angie didn't say anything for a long time after that. The story her mother told was about the man in the mirror, Arthur, her father, and not about the John Doe she had always hated in the photograph on the wall above the couch. "Did he have a green suit?" she asked, before she realized that her mother would consider it an odd question.

Her mother looked startled. "Well, in fact he did," she said. "Double-breasted. It was the suit he wore at our wedding." Another long pause, followed by an audible sigh. "My gosh, he was handsome in that suit." Another long pause. "Pass the macaroni." Then, as she spooned the last of the macaroni onto her plate, she asked, "Who told you about the suit?"

"Never mind," Angie said. "Maybe it's just a thread of an old memory I'm pulling on."

That night, as Angie readied herself for bed, she thought perhaps she might pray for these two men—the old guy at the dump, whose name she didn't know, who still grieved the loss of his little girl, the girl she had seen in the mirror; and her father, not John but Arthur, whose story had intertwined with her own and her mother's in a way very different from what she had thought.

She would pray for her mother too. Somehow the mirror had helped her see her mother in a new light too, not as the victim of a thoughtless jerk who had skipped out on her, but as a courageous survivor of a tragic accident at the printing plant.

She did not know how to pray, so she settled for picturing them in her mind, not as she had seen them in real life but as the mirror had helped her see them, and for the first time she could remember, she wished them well.

She was awakened by blue jays screeching at Old Lady Keillor next door. She went to the window and looked out. The old woman had a watering can and was trying to water the frozen begonias in her flower beds.

Old Lady Keillor had been crazy for as

long as Angie could remember. She'd been surprised when her mother said her father had left her and Joanna in the old woman's care. What that meant was that the old woman had been sane at one time, had been capable enough to care for a toddler and a very young infant. For a long time when Angie was little, she had thought that the old woman's first name was "Mrs." because that was what everybody called her—"Mrs. Keillor." Then one day, when Angie was playing kick the can with the other kids in the neighborhood, Mrs. Keillor had stolen the can and left them all with no way to get home free, so Angie had dropped "Mrs." and substituted "Old Lady" or "Crazyoldlady," making a single word out of it and treating it like a name because it was a better fit than "Mrs." You called somebody "Mrs." when she had dignity. Crazyoldlady Keillor was just nuts. She wore satin slippers in the rain and ran her stick along the public fence railings.

The old lady was wearing the white dress of an ingenue, but it was dirty, torn, threadbare, and much too large for her. It looked as though she'd put it on years ago and then had shrunk inside it as she aged. Along the front were dabs and blotches of paint. She wore a red pillbox hat with a torn veil. And the elbow-length gloves. Angie had no idea how the old lady found these getups, but they didn't suit her. They didn't suit anybody.

Angie went to the chair where her clothes were piled up, dug beneath them for the backpack, and pulled out the mirror. She set the chair near the window and leaned out, angling the mirror so she could get a reflection of Crazyoldlady Keillor.

The image in the mirror was black and white, and it flickered like an old newsreel. There was a long, dark limousine and a crowd of people milling around, waiting for something. Behind the crowd, a bank of searchlights swept the night sky. A theater sign above the marquee said *Roxy*. A dignified-looking man with a pencil-thin moustache stepped out of the crowd and opened the rear door of the limousine. As Angie watched, a gloved hand—long glove—reached out of the rear door and clasped the gentleman's outstretched hand, and then a very young and very glamorous Crazyoldlady Keillor stepped out. Angie could not hear the crowd, but she could see that they were calling out, trying to get the woman's attention. Cameras flashed. The crowd parted like the Red Sea. Somebody with an old-time microphone stepped up. The younger Old Lady Keillor just waved the microphone away and smiled and turned back to the limousine. A Charlie Chaplin–looking man stepped out and strode up to the edge of

the carpet, and the two of them locked arms
and entered the theater. The whole scene
had the quality of an old black-and-white
newsreel, made so long ago that anybody
who was old enough to remember had long
since died. Or gone crazy. The woman in
the mirror was wearing Old Lady Keillor's
pillbox hat and veil.

So there's a story there, Angie thought. *Just
like there was a story in that old man at the
dump.*

Below her in the yard, Crazyoldlady Keillor looked up and caught sight of Angie
looking at her. She stopped watering the
frozen begonias. Angie pulled back inside
and looked back, hoping the old woman
couldn't see her through the glint of the
glass. Then she turned and ran down the
stairs and out to the porch, where she called
Mrs. Keillor by name.

The old woman stopped and looked at

her, an unrecognizing gaze. She doddered over to the fence, stepping into the frozen flower bed with her red satin slippers. She propped herself against the fence with a white-gloved hand.

"Mrs. Keillor, may I talk to you?"

"Go away," Crazyoldlady Keillor said, the gaze stiffening into a glare. "I don't do interviews. Never did interviews."

"I don't want an interview, Mrs. Keillor," Angie said. "I just want to talk to you."

Crazyoldlady Keillor backed away. "You from the *Tribune?* That last lady from the *Tribune* was awful," she said. She gazed into the past at a memory that was clearly disturbing. "Never did interviews, not after that."

"Mrs. Keillor, I'm your neighbor, Angie."

Crazyoldlady Keillor came closer, peering at Angie through a crone's eyes. "Where do you live?" she asked.

"Next door."

"Which one are you again?" Crazyoldlady Keillor said, scrunching up her face and inspecting Angie closely.

"I'm Angela. Angie. You took care of me when I was a little girl, remember? When my father left."

Mrs. Keillor smiled. "Arthur?" she said. "You're Arthur's girl? Nice boy, Arthur."

"Mrs. Keillor, I don't remember my father. Can I talk to you about him?"

"Not through the fence, dear," Crazyoldlady Keillor said, warming to her. "You sure you're not a reporter?" She stepped out of the flower bed and wiped the sides of her satin shoes on the wet, brown grass of the lawn.

Angie went around to the front gate, then up to the porch where the old lady was waiting, holding open a battered screen door. The screen door badly needed paint, and the tacks had come out of one of the corners so the screen swung loose.

"Your father used to fix that for me," Crazyoldlady Keillor said. "He's gone now. Didn't you say he was gone?" They stepped inside. Mrs. Keillor seemed visibly shaken to have someone in her house.

"Oh, my," she said, "it's such a mess in here." She opened the palm of her hand and made a swipe at a dusty table. "Can't get good help anymore, not since the war."

As far as Angie knew, Mrs. Keillor had never had "help."

The room was like an old parlor she'd seen in a museum somewhere. Heavy brocaded wallpaper. Heavy velvet curtains. Heavy cherry furniture, upholstered in velvet to match the curtains. It was a *sitting room*. The curtains were drawn to keep out every sliver of light, so the colors, which were dark enough on their own, seemed like *heavy* colors. Every square inch of every level surface was covered with memorabilia and knickknacks, most of them blanketed in dust. It could have been a badly kept antique store. Or a consignment shop. Or a thrift store. Angie wondered if some of the stuff had little price tags still attached, but she was afraid to look.

Through an open doorway, she could see what might have been an art studio, which explained the dabs and streaks of paint on Crazyoldlady Keillor's dress. She had seen the old woman painting on the porch sometimes in the spring and summer.

She positioned herself so she could look through the door of the studio out of the corner of her eye. A half-finished still life was set up on an easel. Not bad. Surprisingly. "Mrs. Keillor," Angie said, "could you tell me about your dress?" Maybe talking about the dress would calm the old lady's nerves. It was the same dress Angie had seen in the mirror. So were the gloves. In the mirror they had been new.

"My mother made it," Mrs. Keillor said. "I'm wearing it to the Roxy." She went to the closet and took out the mink stole she sometimes wore outside with her nightgown; large tufts of fur fell out as she handled it. "Big premiere," she said. Maybe it was fox fur. Angie wondered about the Roxy; in their town, there wasn't any theater at all, much less a Roxy.

"Were you in pictures, Mrs. Keillor?" Angie asked.

"You can't go, dear," Mrs. Keillor went on. "Not without a press pass. I could get you one if you want. I'll have my agent wire the studio." She put the stole back in the closet, then bustled about, dusting furniture and knickknacks with a badly worn feather duster. She moved things as she worked, and Angie could see clean spots where the items had been.

"Your mother made your dress?" Angie said, nudging the old woman back on track.

Mrs. Keillor smiled. Her face was an older version of the smiling face she had seen in the mirror. "Oh, yes, dear," Mrs. Keillor said. "She sewed it from a picture in a magazine."

Angie changed the subject. "I didn't know you were in the movies."

Mrs. Keillor stood a little straighter and nodded. "Before the talkies."

Angie did some rapid figuring. Mrs. Keillor must be nearly ninety. The limousine in the mirror had been old school, not very evolved from a Model T. As they talked, she looked around the room. Everything seemed to be a couple hundred years old. Mrs. Keillor took off her dress gloves and disappeared into the kitchen, calling out, "Do you want tea, dear?"

"No thank you, Mrs. Keillor," Angie said, loud enough to be heard through the wall. She stood and moved quietly around the room, looking at the memorabilia. She stopped to examine a wall of old black-and-white photographs with ornate frames. One of the photographs was a still shot of the scene at the Roxy that Angie had seen in the mirror.

In one of the photographs, Mrs. Keillor, very young but already dignified, was wearing an antique white lace dress just like the one Angie had seen on herself in the mirror at Christmas. She leaned in and examined the photograph closely. At her throat, Mrs. Keillor was wearing a tiny brooch too small for Angie to make out in any detail, but she wore it precisely the way Angie's reverse image in the mirror had worn the brooch. She wondered if she would find the brooch among the knickknacks on the tops of the tables in the room, or maybe in one of the curio cabinets.

"That was the premiere of my second

film," Mrs. Keillor's voice said softly behind her, startling her out of her reverie about the cameo.

Angie had been so engrossed in the photograph that she had not heard the old lady return. She stepped back, embarrassed for a reason she did not fully understand. She felt as if the photographs, like the mirror in her backpack, were a window into the old woman's soul, and she was aware that she had intruded into a private world to which she had not been invited. "I think your dress was beautiful," she commented. She relaxed and peered again at the photograph.

"My mother made that one too," Mrs. Keillor said. She was carrying a tray with a long-since-worn-out silver tea service. Angie wondered if it was clean. "I hope you take cream and sugar," she said. "I'm like you. I take my tea with cream and sugar."

"I've seen that dress before," Angie said.

Then she corrected herself. "Or one like it." Pause. "Your mother must have been quite a seamstress."

"My mother could do anything," Mrs. Keillor said. She poured the tea. "She was the one who taught me to paint. Do you paint?" She indicated a landscape on the wall. "That's one of mine." Angie examined it closely. The signature on the lower right corner of the painting said *Sybil Sontag*.

"Can you tell me about Arthur?" Angie asked.

"Arthur who?" Crazyoldlady Keillor replied.

"My father. You used to know my father. We lived next door, remember?"

A twinkle came into Mrs. Keillor's eye. "Ah, yes, Arthur. He was your father. What a handsome boy. Had a ruddy face. Had shoulders like an ox. I had a partner like that once, when I worked for the CIA. My gosh, but your father was handsome." Long pause. "I think it was the CIA."

"Tell me about the theater." Angie tried to nudge the old woman back onto psychological terra firma.

Mrs. Keillor resisted the change of topic. "I painted his portrait once. Want to see it?"

"My mother never said anything about a portrait," Angie said.

"I thought about giving it to her," Mrs. Keillor said. "After he left, I mean. But I was afraid it would make her sad."

"I don't think I want to see it now," Angie said. This business with her father was becoming disturbing. Why was he popping up everywhere all of a sudden? But she didn't want to see the picture. "Maybe later," she said, to put Mrs. Keillor off. Then she changed the subject, and the conversation drifted to other things. It was late afternoon when Angie thanked Mrs. Keillor for the tea, excused herself, and made her way home.

Nothing happened next, not for a long time. No miracles, no surprising conversations. Sometimes Angie took the mirror to school, sat in the back of the cafeteria, and puzzled about what she saw. The captain of the football team—a handsome boy, the town's darling—appeared frightened in the mirror, and she found herself trying to find ways to encourage him without letting on that she knew he was afraid. She realized then for the first time what a terrible burden it could be to have the hopes of the town pinned on the back of your football jersey along with your name and number.

She learned that Jan, the town beauty queen, wasn't stuck-up but was painfully shy. In the mirror, Evelyn, the "cootie girl," turned out to be brilliant, an artist with an undiscovered talent but afraid to show her work to anyone because it might just provide another round of taunts and public humiliation. Angie invited Evelyn to visit Mrs. Keillor to talk about art, thinking that perhaps these two lonely souls might discover something good in each other, but Evelyn was afraid of Mrs. Keillor because she was crazy. Angie tried to explain that someone who was crazy might still have gifts to give the world—in this case, painted landscapes that showed remarkable subtlety of form and light. (It was only in retrospect that Angie realized that even the ability to pay attention to such things as subtlety of form and light might be a gift that Mrs. Keillor had somehow given her, just as the ability to notice the tiny gestures of the old man at the dump was a gift she had received—somehow—from the mirror, or from whoever had dropped the mirror into her life.)

Angie herself went to see Mrs. Keillor often. During their visits, Mrs. Keillor would prattle on contentedly, more lucid at some times than others. Sometimes she talked about the old movie stars as though they were still alive. "Mr. Chaplin's a genius," she said once. She had been there the day they started filming *Dough and Dynamite.* "He's the director, and"—she paused for dramatic effect—"he also plays the lead role. Don't know how he does that. I'm supposed to play Madame La Vie, the baker's wife, but I've broken my leg. Norma Nichols is my understudy." Long pause. Then, unexpectedly returning to the present, she added, "We had understudies in those days."

As she talked, Mrs. Keillor handed Angie pictures from a box, one at a time, to look at. "I was a doll, a real knockout, I'll tell you that," she said, smiling, pleased to have someone who would take the time to listen to her story and believe that she had at one time really been a doll, a real knockout.

"What happened between you and Hollywood, Mrs. Keillor?" Angie asked, but as soon as she said this, she regretted it.

"Oh, it was the war, dear," Mrs. Keillor said. "I had to do my little part. Everybody did. My mother was a mechanic, like the queen."

"What did you do, Mrs. Keillor?"

"I can't tell you that, dear," Mrs. Keillor said. Then she relented. "I was a spy, dear." She patted Angie on the hand. "That's what they did with starlets in those days. Made us into spies. I worked for the CIA, strictly hush-hush." She put a bent finger to her leathered lips. "A slip of the lip can sink a ship."

"A spy?" Angie said incredulously.

"Oh, yes, dear. In Paris. On the Riviera. I had a garret on a street near that tower."

"The Eiffel Tower," Angie said, helping.

Mrs. Keillor bent in conspiratorially close. "My cover was that I was an art student. That's where I learned to paint. Had a studio above a restaurant. I don't remember the name. But it was Paris. Definitely Paris. Or maybe some other place. I'm sure it was in France. We had sausages, you know."

Angie did not know what to make of this odd reminiscence. "You worked for the CIA?" she asked.

"Oh, no, dear," Mrs. Keillor replied. "The French resistance. I was a contact in a bakery shop, and I ran messages back and forth between two top-secret cells." Long, nostalgic pause. "They made a movie about that. I played myself."

"Is that true?" Angie asked—a rhetorical question.

"Oh, yes, dear," Mrs. Keillor said. "Arthur McCracken was my leading man. Did you ever see Arthur McCracken? My gosh, but he was handsome."

Angie reached out and touched the old woman on the back of the hand and was startled that her skin was as thin and brittle as oil paper. "I'm sorry, Mrs. Keillor, but I think I'd better go now." She stood and stepped toward the door.

"That's alright, dear," Mrs. Keillor said, looking up. "Thank you for the tea."

Mrs. Keillor died in October. Angie had watched her chasing blue jays out of her garden, but for two or three days she had been missing, staying inside, Angie thought, because of the cold.

She knocked on the door but was met by a stranger in a nurse's uniform.

"I'm Angie. I live next door. Is she alright?"

"We're losing her," the nurse whispered,

stepping back so Angie could pass by her into the sitting room. "We've sent for her son. He's driving out from Cincinnati."

There was a long pause. The nurse set down her clipboard and looked at Angie, glad to have someone to talk to. "She's lived quite a life," she said, shaking her head. Angie looked around the sitting room. The curtains had been drawn back to let in light; she guessed that was the nurse's doing. "She was a surgeon back in the day," the nurse continued, "one of the first women doctors ever to work on the front lines of a war."

Angie murmured something about how that was one she hadn't heard, then went into the old woman's bedroom. Mrs. Keillor's eyes were closed, and she was breathing slow and deep, the breathing of a sleeping cat. Angie touched the brittle oil-paper skin on the old woman's hand. Mrs. Keillor looked up, barely able to open her eyes. When she saw who it was, she smiled. "I want you to have something, dear," she said in a voice so low and thin Angie had to bend close to make it out.

What Mrs. Keillor wanted her to have was the portrait of her father, Arthur. To Angie's immense puzzlement, it was the same painting the mirror had shown on her family's living room wall at Christmas. The man in the painting was indeed handsome, as the old woman had said, but what drew Angie to his face wasn't his good looks as much as the impression of strong character she saw. The painting had been done before the accident had cost him his hand. In an odd way, it helped her put a kind of frame around her father, and within that frame she could see more clearly why he had left. Here was a man who had made a terrible, difficult choice under pressures Angie discovered she could understand only by a movement of empathy. Her great anger at him for leaving was precisely what had kept her from making sense of that choice, and while from her perspective it would always be a wrong choice, in her head she also played and replayed her mother's caution that she had not lived long enough to be her father's judge.

In the portrait, he was seated. He wore the same green double-breasted suit she had seen in the mirror. In the bottom right corner of the painting, in neat lettering, she saw the artist's signature, *Sybil Sontag.*

"Thank you, Mrs. Keillor," Angie said. At that moment, it didn't seem right to ask who Sybil Sontag was.

Mrs. Keillor's son didn't arrive until the following day. By then Mrs. Keillor was gone. She had slipped away in her sleep. She did not die alone. On a chair beside her bed, all that last night, sat Angela McCracken.

Christmas day dawned cold and hard. The family's meager fortunes were hardly better than they had been the year before. Angie and her sister both worked Christmas jobs, but even so, they still had to scrounge for presents. This year they had made do, making presents for each other out of what they had.

Angie gave her mother the portrait Mrs. Keillor had painted of her father. Her mother found a nail and measured the space on the wall above the couch.

"So who painted that?" Joanna asked, picking up the painting so she could get a closer look at the artist's signature in the lower right corner.

"Mrs. Keillor did," Angie said.

Joanna shook her head. "Got somebody else's name on it."

Her mother took the painting and hung it on the nail. "*Sybil Sontag* was Mrs. Keillor's alias during the war. She had to paint under an alias because . . ."

Angie finished the sentence: ". . . the Germans would've recognized her stage name."

"That's right," Angie's mother said. She handed Angie a package addressed to her. "She gave me this last summer. She said she wanted you to have it." Neatly folded inside the package was the antique lace dress. Laid on top, there was a note: "Have your mother fix your hair in a French braid, and think of me and Paris." It was signed, *Sybil Sontag.*

She looked at her mother. "You don't know how to fix a French braid."

"Put the dress on," her mother said. "Then try me."

The combination of the lace dress and the

French braid was lovely, simple—achingly like the girl she had seen before in the mirror. "Where'd you learn to do that?" she asked her mother.

"Katherine taught me," her mother said.

"So who's Katherine?" Joanna wanted to know.

It was Angie who replied: "Katherine was Mrs. Keillor's first name." For all her drifting mental states, Mrs. Katherine Keillor had somehow managed to maintain her dignity.

On Christmas night Angie was left alone in the house with the tree, the gifts, and the ornaments. Her mother went to work at the diner. Her sister washed the dishes and then took off with her boyfriend. Angie went to the bathroom to inspect herself in the lace dress in the mirror. It was beautiful, lovely, but oddly incomplete, she realized, because it needed the carved ivory cameo at the throat.

She went to the kitchen for a cup of coffee, and then settled down on the couch to view the glowing tree and the ornaments.

From the low angle of the couch she saw a single package behind the tree, a present they had overlooked. It was a familiar box, the size of a small book, wrapped in what looked like reused paper and a badly crumpled ribbon. She picked it up. Turned it over. It was the same box, same wrapping, same weight, uneven on one end. It looked exactly like it had the year before, right down to the crumpled ribbon and the reused tape. On the back, in the identical place, the handwritten tag said "McCracken."

What she saw when she opened the box hardly surprised her, but until the day she died she would wonder how it had gotten there. She took the hand mirror to the window to get better light. Held it up. Looked at it again, and nearly fainted. In the oval frame of the mirror, she saw the Christmas tree behind her—dark, bare, stripped of its lights and ornaments.

She held the mirror up again, this time angling it so she could see the tree and its reflection at the same time. The tree in the mirror was bare; the tree in the room was covered by softly glowing lights. She made a slow rotation around the room, checking everything in the oblique angle of the glass.

In the mirror, instead of Mrs. Keillor's oil painting of her father, there hung a black-and-white photograph of John Doe, a man she had never wanted to see again.

She went into the bathroom and pulled the chain on the bare bulb that hung over the sink, then looked at herself in the two mirrors, angling the hand mirror so she could see both reflections at the same time. The girl in the mirror had an open, angry sore on her cheek. While Angie now wore the antique lace dress, the girl in the mirror wore jeans and a T-shirt. She smiled at the face. The girl in the mirror scowled back, angry at the world, her face possessed by a don't-touch-me-or-I'll-take-you-down look that Angie thought must be the definition of *sullen*. The look was distressing to see, but it helped her see herself, somehow, as others had seen her. She brushed her hair back with her fingers, and the image repeated the gesture exactly. She reached to her own cheek, its skin healed now, and the face in the mirror flinched in pain.

A year ago the mirror had sent her on some strange journey; now it was telling her to reflect back on where she had come from.

She looked again at the two images. Things

had reversed, but not perfectly so. There was the hair. There was the dress. There was the change in her eyes from hard and sullen to . . . she didn't know what, but not that. The only thing missing in this odd transformation was the carved ivory cameo brooch.

The day after New Year's she set about to clean the house—left alone by her mother and sister. She cleared the ornaments and lights from the tree, packed them away, loaded the tree into the trunk of the car, and drove out to the Joseph McCracken Refuse Facility, her uncle's memorial dump. The old man was there, like he was every year, grabbing Christmas trees and tossing them up on the same old bonfire. She pulled her car up and got out, went around to help with the tree. "One, two, three, pull."

Then she moved the car and came back

to lend the old man a hand while there was still light. "One, two, three, pull. One, two, three, pull." It went on like that for an hour until finally, at twilight, there was a lull. Together they leaned against the side of his old truck, breathing clouds of mist in the cold air.

He reached into his pocket and took out a battered candy bar, broke it, and handed her half. "I didn't think you'd come," he said.

She bit down on the candy, hard from the cold but still good.

"I got coffee in my truck," he said. He dug around for a battered old thermos. He got out two cups and took off his mittens before he poured. He poured one and handed it to her. Poured the other, picked it up, cupped his hands around it to warm them from the steaming liquid inside. His left hand was missing three fingers.

"I brought you something," he said. He reached into his pocket and pulled out an old red bandana. Folded inside she found a beautifully carved ivory cameo brooch. The girl in the cameo wore her hair in a French braid. In tiny numbers, the bottom edge of the cameo was inscribed with her birthday; the inscription on the top was her name, Angela. "I had it inscribed the day you were born," he said, "but I was saving it to give you on your eighteenth birthday."

She reached out and laid her hand on the old man's shoulder. "Daddy," she said, "don't you think it's about time you came home?"

Somehow the loveliest thing about Christmas was the cleanup.

Jerry Camery-Hoggatt is Professor of New Testament and Narrative Theology at Vanguard University. He is the author of a variety of books in a range of genres, including *Irony in Mark's Gospel: Text and Subtext*, *Speaking of God: Reading and Preaching the Word of God*, *Grapevine: The Spirituality of Gossip*, and *Reading the Good Book Well: A Guide to Biblical Interpretation*. He also wrote an illustrated children's version of *When Mother Was Eleven-Foot-Four*.

Every Christmas Jerry and his family fill their house with poinsettias and the biggest Christmas tree they can find.

Spend Christmas with the family

A WORTHAM FAMILY CHRISTMAS

Till
Morning
Is NIGH

Leisha Kelly
BESTSELLING AUTHOR OF *EMMA'S GIFT*

Amidst the uncertain economic times of the 1930s, the Wortham family discovers the peace of Christmas through a new family tradition.

ℛ Revell
a division of Baker Publishing Group
www.revellbooks.com
Available wherever books are sold

An enchanting

Christmastime journey

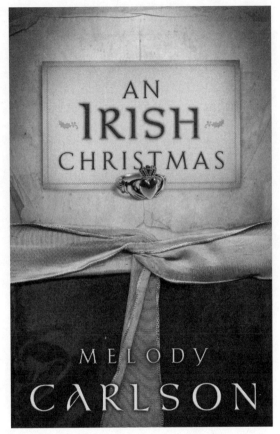

Travel to the hills of Ireland with prolific author Melody Carlson and uncover a captivating story of love, deception, and secret passions in the tumultuous 1960s.

ℛ Revell
a division of Baker Publishing Group
www.revellbooks.com
Available wherever books are sold